A NOTE TO PARENTS

When your children are ready to "step into reading," giving them the right books—and lots of them—is as crucial as giving them the right food to eat. **Step into Reading Books** present exciting stories and information reinforced with lively, colorful illustrations that make learning to read fun, satisfying, and worthwhile. They are priced so that acquiring an entire library of them is affordable. And they are beginning readers with an important difference—they're written on four levels.

Step 1 Books, with their very large type and extremely simple vocabulary, have been created for the very youngest readers. **Step 2 Books** are both longer and slightly more difficult. **Step 3 Books,** written to mid-second-grade reading levels, are for the child who has acquired even greater reading skills. **Step 4 Books** offer exciting nonfiction for the increasingly proficient reader.

Children develop at different ages. **Step into Reading Books,** with their four levels of reading, are designed to help children become good—and interested—readers *faster.* The grade levels assigned to the four steps—preschool through grade 1 for Step 1, grades 1 through 3 for Step 2, grades 2 and 3 for Step 3, and grades 2 through 4 for Step 4—are intended only as guides. Some children move through all four steps very rapidly; others climb the steps over a period of several years. These books will help your child "step into reading" in style!

For Rambling Mike Haag

Library of Congress Cataloging-in-Publication Data
Schade, Susan.
Toad on the road / by Susan Schade and Jon Buller.
p.   cm. – (Step into reading. A Step 1 book)
Summary: A freewheeling toad takes his friend Cat and other animal friends on a spirited driving adventure, always observing safe practices.
ISBN 0-679-82689-0 (pbk.) – ISBN 0-679-92689-5 (lib. bdg.)
[1. Automobile driving–Fiction.   2. Toads–Fiction.   3. Animals–Fiction.   4. Stories in rhyme.]   I. Buller, Jon.   II. Title.   III. Series: Step into reading. Step 1 book.
PZ8.3.S287To   1992
[E]–dc20   91-4246

Manufactured in the United States of America   25 26 27 28 29 30

STEP INTO READING is a trademark of Random House, Inc.

Step into Reading

TOAD
ON THE
ROAD

By Susan Schade
and Jon Buller

A Step 1 Book

Random House 🏠 New York

I love to drive!
I am a Toad.
Here I come—
Toad on the road!

Hands on the wheel.

Eyes on the road.

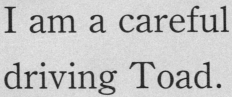

I am a careful
driving Toad.

Hello, Cat.

Hop inside.

I will take you
for a ride.

Seat belt on?

Here we go!

Not too fast,

not too slow.

Take a left.

Take a right.

Stop when you come
to the traffic light.

Stop on red.

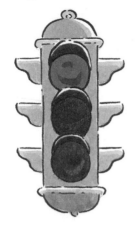

Go on green.

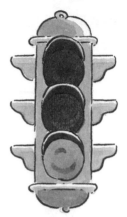

Drive in the car wash.

Come out clean.

The gas is low.

We get a fill-up.

We buy some stuff.
They add the bill up.

We get a flat.

We pump it up.

We give a ride
to our friend Pup.

Cat is hungry.

Stop for lunch.

Sip and slurp.

Chew and munch.

I see Pig
on the bus.

Get off, Pig,

and come with us.

Drive and shop.
Load the trunk.

On the roof rack
put more junk.

Drive them here,
drive them there.

I can drive them
anywhere!

Drive-in
movies,

magic shows,

bowling
alleys,

rodeos.

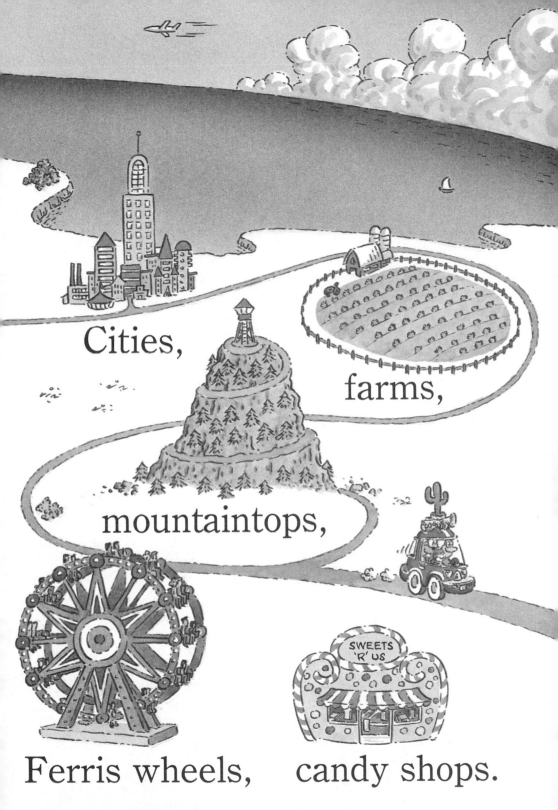

Cities, farms,

mountaintops,

Ferris wheels, candy shops.

Where are we now?
We don't know.

We don't care.

We just GO!